Alfred Simmons

The History of the Parish of All Saints, Poplar

Alfred Simmons

The History of the Parish of All Saints, Poplar

ISBN/EAN: 9783744679398

Printed in Europe, USA, Canada, Australia, Japan

Cover: Foto ©ninafisch / pixelio.de

More available books at **www.hansebooks.com**

THE HISTORY

OF THE

𝔓arish of

ALL SAINTS, POPLAR.

Compiled by

ALFRED SIMMONS.

———————

LONDON:

PRINTED AND PUBLISHED BY THOMAS & BOUTTELL,

46, HIGH STREET, POPLAR.

———

1870.

HISTORY OF POPLAR.

THERE is, probably, no single parish within the area of the metropolitan boundaries which has, in bygone days, been so eminently and intimately connected with the Great City and its interests as the parish, formerly the hamlet, of Poplar. The records preserved in the archives of the place afford a wide scope for historical research ; and whilst many of the events related in the manuscripts are somewhat of the usual formal character, their tedium is frequently dispelled by the discovery of amusing, singular, and in some cases extremely novel incidents. The student is, however, amply repaid at the conclusion of his researches, inasmuch as he has the satisfaction of knowing that he has been enabled, by the exercise of persistent efforts to chronicle the actions of many of those whose names have become household words throughout the country— nay, throughout the world ; whose names must be associated with the noblest of the land ; whose noble deeds have won for them the reverence of succeeding generations ; and whose memories will be cherished in the hearts of myriads of the children of men. Who, in scanning the pages of history, has not repeatedly had his attention arrested by references to " Blackwall Yard," the, at one time, " most considerable ship-building establishment in the kingdom ?" Who, in whatever sphere he may have passed his days, has not heard of the famous "East and West India Docks ?" Who, in his perigrinations eastward of London, has not had his curiosity aroused by the presence of the ancient church erected by the old East India Company ? We feel, therefore, that we are not exceeding the bounds of justice by stating that the parish of All Saints, Poplar, by means of its public and private marine and mercantile establishments, by means of its extensive manufactories, and by the aid of its wealthy inhabitants, has been one of the very bulwarks of the country, and has materially aided in placing Great Britain among the foremost nations of the world.

The name of the parish, according to the renowned "Survey" edited by Mr. Strype, derived its origin from the "multitude of poplar trees growing within and around its boundaries," especially the western portion, where, until very recently a considerable number were still to be observed. The redoubtable "Strype" has truly been beaten with many stripes by contemporary historians for attaching any importance to this circumstance ; but, although these persons have challenged the truth of Mr. Strype's asseverations, we know of none who has propounded as likely a theory, or who has produced satisfactory proofs to the contrary ; and as there is, and probably ever will be, much doubt on the subject, and as Mr. Strype's statement of origin, if not "probable," cannot nevertheless be disproved, we are content to accept that statement as a fact. Regarding the events concerning the parish there is, happily, more reliable information ; and leaving the "possibilities" to those whose desire it may be to deal with them, we will proceed to narrate that which is undoubted, and must be placed amongst the "infallibilities."

By recurring to ancient manuscripts it is discovered that the reversion of the "manor of Popelar" was, in 1396, granted by William of Wykeham (Bishop of Winchester), Sir Aubrey de Vere, and other personages, to the Abbey of "St. Mary de Graces," which abbey is stated to have been situate in close proximity to the Tower of London. For many years succeeding the dissolution of monasteries the manor remained vested in the Crown. Eventually, it was granted to a number of "gentlemen, trustees of the City of London," and by these it was sold to Sir John Jacob. It does not appear when or how the reversion changed hands, but in the next record that is known as referring to the "hamlet" it is stated that in 1558 it was conveyed by Dame Bridget Gardye to Sir Francis Jopson ; again in 1583 it was conveyed by John Hampson, a descendant of the latter, to Thomas Fanshawe ; from Thomas Fanshawe it passed, in 1588 to Edward Elliott. This person retained it until 1620, when it became the property of one John Wyllyams, who obtained a fresh grant of it from the Crown in that year ; and in 1637 sold it to Robert Hooker. Since that time many private individuals have successively become possessors of the reversion of the manor, and in 1842 it belonged to James Humphries, Esq., with whom, or with whose family, it remains at the present day. The manor lands descend according to the custom of gavel-kind.

The manor-house of the parish has for many years been held separately from the demesne. It is stated to have been formerly possessed and occupied by Sir Gilbert Dethick, and then by Sir William Dethick, his son, both of whom were successively garter-king-at-arms. The house was originally a large wooden building, and was situated near the site of the present erection, namely, on the north side of the East India Dock Road. In 1810 it was reported to be in a very dilapidated and dangerous condition; and, in consequence, was demolished, and the present building reared near its site. Until recently the new building was in the occupation of Mr. Thomas Westhorp. Whilst this gentleman resided there a fire broke out in the drawing-room, which destroyed a number of valuable paintings and other articles. At the present time the house, which is a very commodious one, and surrounded by an extensive garden, is held under a rental by Mr. M. Corner, surgeon. A portion of the garden-ground attached to the manor-house was purchased in 1840 by the late Mr. George Green, and he erected thereon an elegant parsonage-house as a residence for the ministers of Trinity Chapel, East India Dock-road.

The hamlet of Poplar and Blackwall was, prior to the year 1817 one of the Tower Hamlets annexed to Stepney. It is recorded in manuscripts preserved by the parish officials that in the year 1655, and again in 1673, the inhabitants of "the hamblett called Poplar, wherein is also Blackwall," made a vigorous attempt to get a separation from Stepney The endeavour however appears to have so signally failed, that the then dignitaries of the parish were unwilling to renew the effort ; and it was not until 1724, when the commissioners appointed to obtain the erection of fifty new churches made a proposal to join the hamlet to "the new parish of Limehouse," that the ardour of the parishioners was again aroused. It was then considered that the annexation to Limehouse would be prejudicial to the hamlet; and at a town-meeting held on the 4th of August (1724) a number of gentlemen were delegated to attend the Board of Commissioners, and to urge, "to the best of their ability" the objections against "joyning the hamblett" with Limehouse, and also to endeavour to obtain permission to "keep the hamblett entire to itself." The deputation were successful in preventing the annexation to Limehouse, but the endeavour to secure a disunion with Stepney was a total failure. Again the enthusiasm of the "separationists" appears to have received an effectual damper, for nothing further is mentioned of the subject until nearly a century had elapsed. In 1815 it is recorded that "in consequence of the very great increase of population in the hamlet, occasioned by the formation of the East and West India Docks, the inhabitants again bestirred themselves to effect a separation; and on the 13th September a public meeting was held at the Town-hall to deliberate on the propriety of an application to Parliament for an Act to form the hamlet into a parish." It was resolved at this meeting to present a memorial embodying the views of the parishioners, and to present it at the proper quarter as "early as convenient." The petitioners firstly laid their memorial before the Bishop of London, who cordially acquiesced in their proposals; and, with his Lordship's assistance a commutation of fees was amicably arranged with the Rev. Thomas Barneby, rector of Stepney. It is stated that the hamlet was called upon during the ten years previous to 1815 to contribute towards the maintenance of Stepney Church, "which was entirely useless to the inhabitants," no less than £7,000; and it is scarcely to be wondered at that a matter of so important a nature should somewhat arouse this enthusiasm. The parishioners strenuously battled with all their difficulties, which appear to have been innumerable, and were eventually rewarded with success. The "Local Act" passed the House of Commons in the early part of 1817, and in the course of that year it received the Royal Assent. The expenses of obtaining the Act amounted to considerably more than £1,400. Much rejoicing followed the successful termination of the agitation, and the first "vestry-meeting of the parish of Poplar" took place in the Town Hall on the 8th of July, 1817.

It may be interesting to mention a most curious story told of a woman named Mary East, who lived in Poplar a few years prior to the events just recorded. It is said that Mary East had a "sweetheart" who, as a penalty for highway robbery, was transported for life. By some means Mary became acquainted with another woman who, like herself, had been "disappointed in love." These two determined to migrate from their own village, and to take up their abode in a place where neither were known, and it was agreed that one (to be determined by lot) should assume the dress of a male, and that they should reside together as man and wife. It fell to the lot of Mary to "transform herself into a man" and to enact the part of husband. She assumed the name of James

Howes. After residing at several country villages they found their way to Poplar, and purchased the White Horse public house in High-street. Mary, alias James, was landlord of the White Horse for upwards of thirty years. She took an active part in parish politics, served two parish offices, and attended the justices' court as a juryman. She served the office of Head-borough of Poplar under the name of "James Howes" in 1744. In 1752 she was elected Overseer of the poor ; and when obliged to own her sex, was in nomination for the office of "Churchwarden of the hamlet of Poplar and Blackwall." Her signature, in a good bold hand, appears on the records of the proceedings of the inhabitants in many instances. In the year 1750 a Mrs. Bentley, a woman who had known Mary from infancy, thought the secret of her metamorphosis a profitable scheme to build a project on ; she accordingly sent to Mary demanding a sum of £10, with a threat that if she refused the money she would discover her sex. Fearful of discovery, Mary complied with the demand. Fifteen years afterwards the woman made a second demand, with like success. Flushed with the prosperity of her scheme she sent again for another £10. Mary, not having the money by her, sent £5. At this time Mary's " wife" died, and Mrs. Bentley determining not to let the opportunity slip, attempted a new plan to enrich herself. She hired two ruffians to aid her designs. A mulatto, named William Barwick, she engaged to appear in the garb of a police officer ; and another was to perform the office of parish constable. These men she sent to the White Horse, and having arrived there they accused Mary of a theft committed some years previously, threatening her that unless she presented them with some money they would expose her deception. Poor Mary, although knowing her own innocence, became exceedingly alarmed, and gave them a cheque for £100 upon a Mr. Williams, a next door neighbour, which they accepted, and made off. Mary, however, determined to submit to this extortion no longer, and resuming the habit of her sex, published the incidents already alluded to, and caused a search to be made for the men. Barwick was arrested, and was tried at Hicks'-hall on the 21st of October, 1766. He was sentenced to four years' penal servitude, and in addition thereto was ordered to be placed in the pillory four times. His accomplice was never discovered. Mary then retired into private life, to live on a decent competency which she had acquired during her 30 years' *landlordism.* She died in May, 1780, and was buried in Poplar Chapel-yard, where a monument to her memory is still to be seen. In the burial-book of the Chapel is the following entry : "Mary East, the woman-man, of Poplar, buried at Poplar, June 4, 1780."

Inseparable from a writing purporting to be a correct historical review of the parish, is a statement of proceedings relating to the East India Company's Chapel, situate on the north side of High-street. The Chapel is a cement-covered brick-built edifice. It has a small turret and clock at the western end; the interior consisting of a nave, chancel, and aisles. The Chapel originally had north, south, and west galleries, but these have recently been removed. The precise date of erection is unknown. There is a reference in the Company's books about the year 1640 to an application made by the inhabitants of the "hamlet of Poplar" for a piece of ground on which to erect a chapel ; and as it appears that the application was granted, there is little doubt that its foundation took place very shortly afterwards ; in fact, in a report of a committee appointed by Parliament in 1650 to make a survey of the locality it is mentioned that "a chapel is being builded in the hamlet." In 1652 a memorial is recorded to have been laid before the East India Company in which the inhabitants prayed for "further assistance" (the land having been *presented* to the hamlet), and the Council generously responded by giving a donation of £200 towards completing the edifice. The remainder of the funds were subscribed by the residents of the hamlet; and in the list of subscribers appear the names of Gilbert Dethick, Esq. (£100), Maurice Thompson, Esq., Sir Henry Johnson, and other influential persons. The edifice was erected for about the sum of £2,200. "The chappell was almost entirely ruined" by the great storm of 1703, and the inhabitants again appealed for assistance from the East India Company, alleging as their reason for so doing that "the town was very much encumbered," and that the residents were unable to defray the expense of effecting the repairs. The Company promised to help them, but on application being made for the sum solicited the officials were informed that the Council had determined to "withdraw the promise." The inhabitants were terribly chagrined at this. It is affirmed that the work had already been done and that "the sum of £104 was due to the churchwarden on account thereof." An old minute book states that "although the repairs were performed chiefly at the repeated instances of Dr. Woodward (the chaplain) and the East India Company, yet since no manner of provision hath been made for defraying the said charges, we think it reasonable that the dues should be appropriated to the defraying of the said charges." No further mention is made of the matter, and it is presumed that in accordance with the foregoing minute the "said charges" were defrayed by the "said dues." The hamlet does not appear to have been in a remarkably flourishing state at this period, for in 1706 the churchwarden (Mr. Rolt) was ordered to purchase "a velvet pawl (or pawls) for the use of the town, and that interest be paid for the money *advanced* for the purchasing of the said pawl (or pawls)." As a means of ensuring payment of the loan for this extensive business transaction, the pawl (or pawls) were ordered to be given into the custody of the churchwarden, with implicit directions that if "any forreigne or other pawl (or pawls) or gowns should be brought into the hamlet, he demand the same fees as if those belonging to the towne had been used." In 1721 application was made by Dr. Landon (the minister) to the East India Company to put the chapel into "a proper state of repair, the same being again out of order." The Company consented to do so on "the understanding that no misapprehension should arise respecting the right to the chappell and presentation of the minister." The inhabitants agreed to this provision, and it was promised "that the Company will keep it for ever in a state of repair." In 1774 the chapel again required to be repaired, and the inhabitants having petitioned the Company, and "reminded them of their former promise," the repairs were immediately ordered to be done. In the following year the burial ground was enlarged 30 feet. The chapel and burial ground were never consecrated. In 1803 the edifice underwent a thorough "beautifying." The late J. Perry, Esq., presented the organ, with an endowment of five guineas per annum for ever. There are many curious but excellent monuments, both in the chapel and ground. Over the vestry door is a magnificent monument in memory of "Captain Philip Worth, commander in the Hon. East India Company's service, who died March 24th, 1742, in his 47th year; also to Elizabeth, his widow, who died July ye 5th, 1754, in the 60th year of her age." In the north aisle is a beautiful marble monument, by Flaxman, "In memory of George Stevens, Esq., who cheerfully devoted a portion of his life and fortune in the illustration of Shakespere." Stevens is represented in bas-relief sitting before the bard's bust, which he is ardently contemplating. On the eastern wall is a tablet in memory of " Susannah, widow of John Hoole, Esq., auditor of Indian Accounts, and known in literary circles as the translator of Tasso and Ariosto ; died 5th of April, 1808, aged 80, having survived her amiable husband nearly five years." In the south aisle is a monument to John Perry, of Moor Hall, Essex, formerly shipbuilder, of Blackwall, and founder of the Commercial Docks." He died July 5th, 1824, aged 56. There are numerous tablets and monuments commemorating the decease of respected inhabitants and others, on the walls of the building. In the cemetery is a stone in memory of Captain William Curtis, "who left by his will £60 per annum, for ever, to apprentice poor children of Poplar, Mile-end, Limehouse, Shadwell, and Ratcliff ; and for an annual sermon to the Trustees in April or May." There is another stone to the memory of " Samuel Jones, Esq., captain in the Navy : he engaged a superior force of the French off Cape Rivella in 1706, and off Beachy Head in 1707, and with signal bravery and conduct put them to flight."

The first chaplain specially appointed for the hamlet of Poplar was the Rev. Thomas Walton ; he was appointed in 1654 by the vicar of Stepney, the Rev. Mr. Greenhill. The Rev. Samuel Peck is said to have followed, and was appointed by the inhabitants in 1670. The third was the Rev. Josiah Woodward, M.A., who was elected in 1690 by the inhabitants " subject to the approval of the Bishop of the diocese." Mr. Woodward resigned in 1711, and a spirited contest arose from the fact of Dr. John Landon and the Rev. Henry Sheppard having been put into nomination for the vacant pulpit. Both gentlemen were much respected, and were eloquent preachers ; Dr. Landon was, however, elected by a large majority. He faithfully officiated for a period of 17 years, and died much lamented in 1728. Dr. Landon was succeeded by the Rev. Dr. Gloster Ridley, who was the first minister appointed under the provisions of the " understanding" with the East India Company. Dr. Ridley's salary was increased to £50 per annum ; his predecessor having enjoyed the handsome income of £25 per year. On the death of Dr. Ridley, which event occurred in 1774, the Rev. John Wheeler, LL.D. was unanimously chosen, and performed his duties with much earnestness for 29 years. In

1803 he was made Prebendary of Westminster ; and on his retirement the Rev. Samuel Hoole, M.A. was elected. On the completion of the parish Church Mr. Hoole was selected to be the first rector of Poplar, and having resigned his chaplaincy to the Company's chapel in 1823, was succeeded by the Rev. Henry Higginson, M.A. The salary was then increased to £500 per annum. Mr. Higginson died suddenly at the parsonage house on the 5th of February, 1848 ; and the living was next conferred upon the Rev. H. Hamilton, M.A., who resigned in favour of the Rev. Mr. Boswell. On the latter gentleman's decease, the Rev. W. J. Jay was appointed, who endeared himself to the whole of the inhabitants. He, however, accepted the living of a church erected in Suffolk by his Royal Highness the Maharajah Dhuleep Singh, with whom Mr. Jay was intimately acquainted, and retired in 1866. At this time Henry Green, jun., Esq., and Edward Coleman, Esq., were constituted trustees for the Bishop of London—Dr. Tait—until arrangements were completed by the India Council and the Ecclesiastical Commissioners, by which the patronage of the living was vested in the Bishop of London for ever. The Rev. J. F. Kitto, B.A.,was then appointed, and this gentleman retains the living at the present time—the income of the minister now amounting to between £300 and £400 per annum. Old things have passed away, however, and the "East India Company's Chapel," as a name, is now no more. The chapel has recently undergone a thorough renovation, and the Bishop of London having assigned to it a portion of the parish, comprising a population of 5,000 inhabitants, it is now denominated " St. Matthias District Church."

Originally there were a number of "East India Company's Almshouses" lying adjacent to the chapel, intended for the occupation of seamen and others who had been disabled, or had by infirmity become unfit for work, whilst in the Company's service. The date of the erection of these houses is not known for certain. Dr. Woodward was of opinion that they were built " when the chapel was founded, or near to the same time ;" but a gentleman, Mr. Wheeler, who is thoroughly acquainted with the documents preserved by the Company relating to the buildings, informed the editor of the " Environs of London," the well-known Mr. Lysons, that they were erected previously to the year 1632. Of the two statements the latter is most probably the more reliable. There was attached to the houses a hospital providing accommodation for 14 seamen, who, by accident or infirmity, were unable longer to remain in the Company's service. These persons received pensions amounting to £6 10s. and upwards per annum, according to the rank of the recipient while in the service. In addition to this they were supplied with " half a chaldron of coals for the winter, and a superadded bounty at Christmas." The Company's "Shipping Committee" usually inspected the almshouses at Christmas-time, and they invariably distributed about £100 amongst the widows and orphans of the seamen who had been in their service. The houses were 22 in number, and in 1802 they were reported to be in so dilapidated a condition as to be " dangerous for the poor people to live in." They were consequently demolished, and others of a much superior description erected in their place. At the same time the dwellings were increased to 56 ; 18 of this number were of a more commodious character, and were reserved entirely for the occupation of invalided commanders and mates, or their widows. In 1866, however, the whole of the occupants were requested to vacate the houses, and received an increased pension from the Company in lieu of house accommodation. Shortly afterwards the Poplar District Board of Works opened negociations for the purchase of the land on which they stood, with an adjoining site facing East India Dock-road. The negociations ended successfully ; the land being purchased for the sum of £12,000, half of which sum was paid by the local board, and the remainder by the Metropolitan Board of Works, on the understanding that, with the exception of a small portion at the south-east corner, the whole be devoted to the purposes of a "Recreation Ground for the people, and that it remain as such for ever." The portion excepted was retained by the Board with a view of erecting thereon a Board-room and public offices. The inscription stone of these buildings was laid by E. Coleman, Esq., on Thursday, the 20th of May, 1869, and at the time of writing they are almost completed, the cost of erecting them being computed at £9,000.

The first important act of the parish officials succeeding the obtaining of the local Act in 1817 was the purchase of "eight acres of ground whereupon to erect a church and parsonage house, and for forming a church-yard," &c. This having been acquired, premiums were offered for plans for a parish church. Thirty-six designs were submitted, and after many " wordy-wars" between the local politicians of the day, the "capital premium" of £100 was awarded to Mr. C. Hollis, who undertook the surveyorship of the building. The erection of the edifice was entrusted to Mr. Thomas Morris, of Poplar. The "first stone" was laid by the then Bishop of London with the customary ceremonials. The following is the inscription on the stone : "The first stone of this parish church of All Saints, "Poplar, in the County of Middlesex, was laid the 29th day of "March, 1821, by the Right Rev. Father in God, William "Howley, D.D., Lord Bishop of London, in the second year of "the reign of his most gracious Majesty George IV. Rev. "Samuel Hoole, A.M., rector ; James Mountague, church- "warden and treasurer ; Thomas Lambert, churchwarden ; "Isaac Ramsay, William Mills, Archibald Ritchie, and William "Edgcumbe, overseers of the poor ; Charles Hollis, architect; "Thomas Morris, builder ; Thomas Horne, vestry clerk." "O Lord our God, all this store that we have prepared to "build thee an house for thine own holy name cometh of thine "own hand, and all is thine own.—1 Chron. xxix. 16." The expense of the ceremony of laying this stone was £437 19s. 8d. The edifice, which is situate on the southern side of East India Dock-road, between Newby-place and Bow-lane, is regarded as one of the most handsome of the metropolitan churches. The subjoined is a professional description : "The portico is of the Ionic order, supported by four columns ; the basement of the tower is rusticated, from whence arises the beauties of the Corinthian order ; above this is the place appropriated for the dial. On this part stands a colonnade of sixteen composite pillars, which has a very pleasing effect ; the entablatures of these columns are ornamented with several circular plinths or bases, gradually diminishing upwards, from the top of which springs a light and beautiful spire, terminating with a vane upwards of 160 feet from the ground. The north and south-western entrances are of the same order as the portico, but the body of the church ill accords with the richness and beauty of the tower and spire. Under the church are cemeteries for the dead . . .' The plinth and area of the western entrance are of granite, the rest of the building of Portland stone. The interior of the church exhibits but few architectural beauties. The pulpit and reading desk are of oak. Some pains were taken to beautify the altar, and with this view two elegant Corinthian columns, enriched with corresponding pilasters of scagliola, in imitation of Sienua marble, are introduced with an ornamental entablature, in the centre of which is placed the royal arms, having on either side the colours formerly belonging to the Blackwall Corps. Under an entablature supported by scagliola, in imitation of Verd antique, is a painted window. The design of the painting (Christ preaching) would appear to be borrowed from Limehouse Church, and is anything but a happy effort of the painter." During the past three years a number of memorial windows have been presented by influential parishioners, which have considerably improved the internal appearance of the church. The tower contains a fine set of ten bells. Around the church are spacious grounds, formerly used as a cemetery, but which are now closed against interments, and are ornamented with flowers and shrubs.

The Church was consecrated on July 3rd, 1823, by the Bishop of London, and the first sermon preached by the Rev. Mr. Hoole, the rector, from the words " And Ezra, the scribe, stood upon a pulpit of wood, which they had made for the purpose." After the sermon the rector delivered the following address :— " Men, Brethren and fellow Christians,—a purpose more solemn and more important can scarcely be conceived than that which brings us together this day. We meet here to found an edifice which we trust will endure for many generations, dedicated to the worship and service of our invisible Creator and constant Benefactor ; an edifice in which the doctrine of the Redeemer of mankind may be faithfully inculcated, the duties of Christian morality earnestly enforced, and the principles of peace, order, and happiness be disseminated among every class of the community. In the prosecution of a work, begun I hope, in the fear of God, let no worldly motive, no private interest, no narrow prejudice intervene to thwart or retard it ; but let us vigorously and honestly persevere in what is at length so auspiciously commenced, with the ardour of hot patriots and with the zeal of Christians ; and let us enter upon this, as upon all our undertakings with fervent supplication to that Supreme Lord of whom and through whom and to whom are all things ; that by His favour and protection this consecrated structure may afford the means of confirming our children and our children's children in the word of truth, and of promoting the salvation of multitudes yet unborn . . . . O Lord God of Heaven and earth, in whose hands are the ways and works of all created things, who, by the secret influence of

Thy Holy Spirit, impartest strength and council to the weak and simple, and bringest to nought the cunning craftiness of the wise, grant us grace to use Thy gifts for Thy glory, that we may not lavish what Thy bounty bestows on empty trifles, nor consume that time nor those talents on things temporal which ought to be devoted to things eternal. Bless these our exertions (for without Thy blessing all human labor must be unavailing), that on this spot a fabric may rise in which Thy sacred name shall be continually adored, Thy divine gospel diligently promulgated, the unspeakable mercy of redemption thankfully commemorated, and that good seed effectually sown which will bring forth fruit to life eternal ; and hasten, O righteous Father, hasten, if it be Thy good pleasure, that happy period when the earth shall be filled with the knowledge of the Lord as the waters cover the sea, when every nation, kindred, and people shall give glory to Thee in the highest, and peace and goodwill reign among men, and the triumphant song of the heavenly host resound from the east and from the west, from the north and from the south, in every language of the habitable world ; blessing and honour and glory be unto Him who sittest upon the throne and unto the Lamb for ever."

The parsonage-house stands opposite to the grand entrance to the church, in Newby-place. The total expenditure on the church, parsonage, burial ground, &c., was a trifle over £33,000. The Rev. Mr. Hoole died in February, 1839, and was succeeded by the Rev. Thomas Bazely, who retired in 1860. The Rev. T. W. Nowell, M.A., is the present rector of the parish. The living is worth about £400 per annum, and is the gift of the Council of Brazenoze College ; the rector's salary and cost of maintaining the church being levied upon the inhabitants in the shape of a Church Rate.

Since the erection of the parish church, however, the population has so rapidly increased that it has been found necessary to establish a number of district churches. At the present time there are six, as follows:—St. Saviour's, Northumberland-street, the Rev. E. Bray ; St. Stephen's, North-street, East India-road, the Rev. E. Elliott ; St. Matthias' (late Poplar Chapel), High-street, the Rev. J. F. Kitto ; Christ Church, Cubitt-town, Isle of Dogs, the Rev. J. Caparn ; St. Luke's, Strafford-street, Millwall, the Rev. J. Hewlett ; and St. Paul's, Cubitt-town, the Rev. W. Carpenter. To each of these a district containing about 5,000 inhabitants has been

apportioned ; but all are under the general supervision of the
Rev. T. W. Nowell, the rector of the parish.

At the extreme south of Poplar parish proper, is a tract of
land known as the " Isle of Dogs." It lies within a bold curve
of the River Thames, and is about three miles in circumference.
The " Island," as it is now generally denominated, is reported
to have acquired its appellation from the circumstance that
Edward II. kept his hounds there, that is to say, those used
when he and his courtiers hunted in Greenwich Park (which
lies immediately opposite, on the other side of the Thames) and
the neighbouring country. The Corporation of the City of
London, however, possess some old manuscripts in which it is
described as the " Isle of Ducks," probably from the fact that
in ancient times it is known that myriads of wild fowl located
themselves there. There is also a story extant which claims to
have originated the cognomen " Isle of Dogs." It is said that
a traveller desired a ferryman, one William Summers, to carry
him from the opposite shore to the Island. The ferryman
obeyed the request, but discovering that his patron had in his
possession a large sum of money, detained him on some
frivolous pretence, and at eventide led him to the marshes and
there " foully murdered him in cold blood." The traveller,
however, had with him a faithful dog, which, unobserved by
the murderer, followed his master and remained by the corpse.
Compelled by hunger the dog prowled about in search of food,
and at length attracted the attention of some persons whose
business led them thither. They followed the dog, and
eventually discovered the mangled body of the unfortunate man.
The murderer was apprehended some time afterwards, and was
executed on the spot where he had enacted his dreadful crime.
It is probable, we think, that the circumstance first narrated
is the true origin of the appellation. The Island, in years
gone by, was celebrated on account of the peculiar richness of
the soil. Strype, in his " Circuit Walk," asserts that oxen
fed upon the marshes had been known to sell for £34 a-piece ;
and he mentions that a butcher residing in Poplar, " adjoyning
the marsh," contracted to supply a club at Blackwall with a
" legge of mutton, every week throughout the year, weighing
not less than 28-lbs. Such legges of mutton to be cut from
sheep fed on the Isle of Dogs marshes ;" and it is added, " the
butcher performed the same." A remarkable phenomenon was
discovered here while the excavations for the West India Docks

were proceeding in the year 1800. About eight or nine feet below the surface of the ground was discovered what had evidently been a portion of a forest. Decayed branches, twigs, and leaves, encompassing huge trunks, perfect in every fibre, yet literally rotted through, were brought to the light of day. The trees appeared to have been uninjured, and had apparently been torn from the soil by their roots. Naturalists have supposed that many centuries since, the spot must have been visited with a terrific cyclone, immediately followed by an earthquake ; and truly by no other theory could so remarkable a discovery be explained. Mr. C. H. Wigram, shipbuilder, of Blackwall, has in his possession some fossil remains which were also found, one of which is stated to be a portion of the tusk of some huge animal. It is about three feet in length, about 4½ inches in thickness, and is in an excellent state of preservation. One historian, in writing of the Isle of Dogs, says, "The cold and swampy character of this marsh would appear repulsive to all thoughts of human habitation, but piety, which in its obsolete modifications, sometimes sought strange recesses, induced an unknown devotee to found a chapel in the midst of the marsh, which is believed to have been dedicated to St. Mary." This chapel was, however, demolished, and on its site erected a building known in these latter days as the "Old Chapel-house Farm." The proprietor of this building set up some claims to antiquity for a portion of the erection, but to practical observers it exhibited few particulars to entitle it to such claims. The lower part of the walls were composed of stones and flint, and it is asserted that about 1790 a Gothic window was removed from the building ; with these exceptions the "Chapel Farm" savoured unmistakeably of recent structure. But, alas ! the place that knew the "Chapel Farm" now knows it no more, for the site was purchased, along with some scores of acres of the adjoining marshes, a few years back by the Millwall Docks Company, and where once the folk of Poplar, and sage anti-quarians "stopped to gaze, and, gazing, admired," appears nothing but a sheet of water, one of the basins of the new Dock Company. But a small portion of the marsh remains to tell the story of what has been, for hundreds of human habi-tations, with tall-spired churches, now cover the face thereof, and what the historian before alluded to considered a situation "repulsive to all thoughts of human habitation," now presents a busy scene of shipyards, factories, wharves, and "houses for folk to live in."

The date of the erection of the first Town Hall for Poplar is not known. There is a minute in an old parish manuscript which states that a "Town meeting" was held in the year 1593 ; and as it is presumed that the business of the "hamlet". was not enacted in the streets, the conclusion must be arrived at that a "Town-house" had sprung into existence prior to the year named. However that may be, it is declared in the not-to-be-doubted "parish record" that a "Town-house" stood in the "highway" near to the site of the present Green Dragon public-house ; and that in the year 1764 a committee was delegated to "survey the old house" with a view of ascertaining the expense of its renovation or re-building. The committee, in a lengthy report, recommended that the "House be entirely re-built." Some opposition appears to have been offered the officials, and the matter was shelved till that date six years. In 1770, therefore, the subject was again mooted, and it was then determined to pull down the old house and to erect another on "part of the ground belonging to the work-house." The amount realised by the poor-rate collection being insufficient to fully carry out the contemplated improvement, a public subscription was opened, and in a few months the "handsome sum of £172 3s. had been subscribed." The building was then completed, and the first meeting was held in "the new Poplar Town Hall" on the 22nd of November, 1771. It was determined to demolish the old poor-house a short time after the erection of the Town Hall ; but a delay of some years took place which is totally unaccounted for in the records. The building of the present workhouse was commenced in 1815, and it was completed in 1817, the total cost being £15,500. The Town-hall was the centre portion of the workhouse building, and would accommodate about 400 persons. According to the writings of the time, Poplar Workhouse, when finished in 1817, was looked upon as a "model establishment ;" but alas! for the farsightedness of the critics of the period. Ere 40 years had winged their flight a certain Poor-law Inspector wrote respecting this same "well ventilated, commodious, and elegant house," that it was "inadequate in size and inefficient in arrangement :" which writing so acted upon the temperaments of the several gentlemen then constituting the Board of Guardians, that they arrived at the conclusion that "a new Workhouse was absolutely necessary." It proved to be a harder matter to convince the ratepayers of the parish that this conclusion was a correct one than had apparently been imagined. Public meetings were held to "protest against the extravagant and unwarrantable expenditure," and, the annual election of Guardians being nigh at hand, it was determined not to allow the opportunity to pass without challenging the Guardians' right to expend £40,000 prior to testing the feelings of those upon whom would fall the burden of providing the money. The consequence of the agitation was that nearly all the members of the Board were in the ensuing election rejected, and eight gentlemen—"the ratepayers' eight," all of whom had pledged themselves to oppose the erection of a new Work-house—returned by a majority of more than 1,000 votes. The newly-constituted Board, however, quickly discovered that additional accommodation was "absolutely necessary," and it was proposed to add another wing to the present workhouse, by which an outlay would have been incurred of £6,300. This proposition was, after many party fights, out-voted ; and it was then determined that the guardians should, before making any alterations or erecting any additions, acquire the freehold of the land on which the Workhouse stood, with a piece of land at the rear belonging to the East and West India Dock Company. The former was purchased of the Trustees of Poplar for £10,000 (which sum included the proprietary of the Workhouse building also), and the latter was parted with by the Dock Company for £2,787. In addition to this the Guardians obtained the lease from the Dock Company of another piece of land adjoining that which had been purchased, and, after a delay of a few months, those gentlemen who had been elected for the osten-sible purpose of opposing the erection of a new House found it necessary to pass a resolution determining to build additions to the workhouse capacious enough to accommodate 808 able-bodied inmates. It is due, by the way, to one or two of the Guardians to state that a strenuous opposition has been offered to the majority, but which proved to be of no avail. Mr. J. W. Morris, of Poplar, was appointed architect, and on the 20th March, 1869, the Board selected from a numerous supply the tender of Messrs. Hill, Keddall, and Waldram, of Kingsland, who contracted to erect the buildings for £32,480. On Wednesday, the 21st of April, 1869, the first stone of the new buildings was laid with the usual ceremony by James Barringer, Esq., the Chairman of the Board of Guardians. The work has been steadily progressing

since that date, and at the time of issuing this sketch the
erections are well-nigh completed. The new buildings consist
of east and west double pavilions with, a chapel, bakehouses,
kitchens, &c. No pretence to architectural beauty or orna-
mentation has been made, the erections being of the ordinary
description of plain brick-work.

The purchase of the Workhouse from the Trustees, however, necessitated the erection of a new Town Hall for the
parish, inasmuch as the Guardians, immediately upon taking
possession of the property, converted the old hall into wards
for the use of the inmates of the Workhouse. The Trustees,
therefore, with the £10,000 paid them by the Guardians determined to build a new Town-hall, combining with it parochial
and other offices, upon a piece of land belonging to the parish
situate in Newby-place, and upon which then stood the old
watch-house and fire-engine station. Negociations were also
opened with the authorities of Brazenoze College, the
Bishop of London, and the Rev. T. W. Nowell, the rector of
the parish, to obtain the site upon which the infants' schools
connected with the Church stood, with a view of extending the
size of the land already possessed by the Trustees. These
negociations were brought to a successful termination, the
authorities agreeing to erect another school in place of the
one to be demolished. The consent of the Charity Commissioners
was then sought and obtained for applying the money to the
purposes named ; and the Trustees, in their turn, appointed
architects (Messrs. A. & C. Harston, of Limehouse), who prepared plans of the buildings. Tenders were then invited, and
sixteen having been submitted, that of Mr. A. Sheffield, of East
India Dock-road, was accepted. Mr. Sheffield's tender was
the lowest, and offered to carry out the works for the sum of
£7,479. The foundation stone was laid on the 28th of February,
1870, by George Guttridge, Esq., the senior churchwarden of
the parish. According to the drawings, the style of archi-
tecture is to be of an Italian character. The principal entrance
is to an open vestibule, with fluted piers, red granite shafts,
and carved capitals ; and above the vestibule will be an open
balcony, the arches of which are to be supported by caryatides.
The vestibule and balcony will be constructed entirely of
Portland stone. The remaining portion of the frontage will be
faced with yellow malm bricks, with a cornice of Portland stone;
with pierced balustrading, finials, strings, and window dressings,

and red granite shafts to the windows of the Town-hall.   The
ground-floor will comprise a Board-room and committee-rooms,
clerks' offices, &c. ; whilst the main (Town) hall will be on the
first-floor.   The dimensions of the hall are 70-ft: in length, by
40-ft. in breadth.   It will have three separate approaches to
the street, i.e., the grand staircase leading to the body of the
hall, and two other staircases leading to the gallery and to the
back of the hall.   The main staircase is to be approached by a
large hall in the centre of the ground floor, exactly opposite the
principal entrance.   It is anticipated that the work will be
completed by about the spring of 1871.

   Several old-established charities continue to be observed in
the parish.   Amongst the most important of these is one
originated in the year 1686 by Mrs. Hester Hawes, or Haines.
This lady |erected almshouses in Bow-lane, a short distance
from the High-street, for the occupation of " six of ye most
antient poore women (widows or maids) of ye hamblett of
Poplar," and endowed the same with £9 per annum for ever.
The houses are in existence and occupied at the present time,
the pensions being paid by the heirs of the late John Stock,
Esq.—Sir H. Johnson, a former proprietor of Blackwall Yard,
left, on his decease in 1680, the sum of £300 for the erection
of " six good and substantial tenements, each tenement to
contain two rooms, with a chimney in each room."   The
dwellings were to be set apart for the occupation of " poore
shipp-carpenters" who had attained the age of " three-score
years or more," and who had laboured for their living in
Blackwall Yard.   The occupiers were to be presented annually
with a blue gown, with the donor's coat of arms thereon, and
were to receive a weekly allowance of 2s. 6d., and an additional "half-a-crown at Christmas-time."   In deference to the
deceased's request, the houses were erected in a thoroughfare
called " Globe-yard ;" but the Earl of Stafford, who married
Sir Henry Johnson's eldest daughter, and became the pos-
sessor of the estate in which the charity was situate, neglected
to pay the poor people their pensions.   In the year 1722 the
Earl disposed of the estate, and the parishioners took steps to
" establish" the charity.   Meetings were held, the matter was
represented to the Earl's successor, and eventually the inhabitants succeeded in their effort.   Since that time the pensions
have been regularly paid by each successive owner of Blackwall
Yard, and at the present time, the Messrs. Green being pro-

prietors of the estate, the poor persons periodically receive the
amount provided by Sir Henry Johnson's philanthrophy.
About forty years ago the old dwellings were demolished and
rebuilt.—John Tell, Esq., by will dated 1742, caused almshouses to be erected at Blackwall for poor watermen who had
served their apprenticeship in the hamlet. The recipients of
this charity were to be nominated by the minister of the place,
or by the churchwardens and overseers. Mr. Tell left no
endowment for the property, but made provision by which £3
per annum is secured to keep the houses in repair.—There
have been numerous bequeathments of sums of money to be
distributed annually in bread to the poor of the parish. Among
these is one by John Perry, Esq., of Blackwall, who, by his
will dated 1772, left the sum of "£200 per annum, to be given
in bread to the poor of the hamlet;" and, in 1805, John
Perry, Esq., son of the former, added to his father's bequeath-
ment the sum of £218, to be devoted to the same purpose.—
A somewhat novel circumstance is recorded to have taken
place at a meeting of the inhabitants held in 1737. It appeared
that the rate-collectors had "fraudulently and unwarrantably
collected the sum of £350" odd from the property owners of the
hamlet; and it was therefore ordered that the sum of £44
sixteen shillings and eightpence should be paid into the hands
of the senior churchwarden, John Pharoah, Esq., for the use
of the hamlet, with instructions that he and the succeeding
churchwardens should "for ever distribute the sum of 12d.
weekly in 2d. loaves" to six poor persons residing in the
hamlet.

It has already been asserted in this history that the old
shipbuilding yard at Blackwall was, in former times regarded
as "the most considerable private shipbuilding establishment
in the kingdom;" and were it necessary this statement might
easily be verified by facts. It is only necessary here, however,
to state that from this yard has emanated nearly the whole of
the world-renowned East India Company's fleet; here has
been built numerous vessels which have done noble work in
establishing that glorious maxim, "Britannia rules the waves;"
and from the dock adjoining the yard were embarked the whole
of the regiments of cavalry sent to the continent of America at
the time when our trans-Atlantic brethren were struggling with
the mother-country for their independence. Such were the
facilities offered at this establishment for speedily embarking

the troops, that it is stated : " embarkation that formerly took three days was here completed in as many hours." In 1720 the property belonged to Sir Henry Johnson & Son, and from the baronet's family it passed to John Perry, Esq., who, in 1789, made a " spacious dock,which was called the Brunswick Dock." The latter was some years afterwards purchased by the East India Dock Company and incorporated in their newly-formed docks. While the yard was in the possession of Mr. Perry a wooden building was erected called " Blackwall Mast-house." It was built for the purpose of laying-up the masts and rigging of vessels used in the service of the East India trade, and was 120-ft. high. Therein were placed gear and machinery for masting and dismasting the ships, and by this scheme the old-fashioned plan of erecting sheers on the decks of the vessels was rendered unnecessary. The usual time taken to mast a vessel was about two days and a half; but by the mast-house and its machinery this task could be completed in less than four hours, and with about one-half the number of men. The first ship masted at the " House" was the " Lord Macartney," the event taking place on the 25th October, 1791. This building was demolished in 1864. Several royal visits have been paid to the establishment, and an amusing story is told of his Majesty George III. The king went to Blackwall to review some troops prior to their embarkation. It was on a beautiful summer day, and a large concourse of people was assembled. The tale is told by an anonymous writer in the following terms :—"A jolly tar, a little more than " three sheets in the wind," but " brim full of loyalty," and, conse-quently regardless of the laws of etiquette or decorum, deigned to " approach his most gracious Majesty's royal person" armed with a pewter pot filled with Barclay's porter, which he had purchased at a neighbouring public-house. Jack " tongued his quid," " unshipped his sky scraper," " hitched up his canvas," and, approaching his Majesty, presented him with the humble draught, at the same time expressing a hope that he would not refuse to drink with "an honest true blue." The king, as may be supposed, was for the moment astounded at the impudence of the "jolly sailor;" but Jack was not to be beaten off, and a second time he importuned his Majesty to "take a sip." His Majesty, finding that the remonstrances of his courtiers were useless, good-humouredly took the pewter tankard from the hands of the importunate tar, and, giving for a toast, "The Army and the Navy," drank deep of the invigorating beverage, then, returning the remains to Jack, accompanied with a golden coin of the realm, desired he would go and buy more beer, that he with his shipmates might drink "Success to the campaign, and long life to the King and Queen"—a request which Jack, no doubt, obeyed with more zest and alacrity than when ordered to mount the mainmast on a winter's day. George Green, Esq., succeeded Mr. Perry in the proprietary of "Blackwall Yard," and whilst in possession of Mr. Green the yard was divided, and a large portion purchased by Messrs. Money Wigram & Sons. On the demise of Mr. Green the portion retained was left by will to his two sons Henry and Richard, and the latter having followed his sire to the tomb it now belongs to Mr. Henry Green's family.

The construction of the "West India Docks" was commenced on the 12th July, 1800, and they were finished at the latter end of 1802. The scheme was projected by the late R. Milligan, Esq., a West India merchant. The docks are situate towards the southern extremity of the parish, and extend in a direct line from east to west, having entrances at Blackwall and Limehouse. The land purchased by the Company amounted to 204 acres. There is a basin at either entrance to the docks, the one at the Blackwall entrance having a water area of $6\frac{3}{4}$ acres, and the one at the Limehouse entrance an area of $1\frac{1}{2}$ acres. These basins communicate outwardly with the Thames by means of locks 46 and 36 feet wide respectively. Inwardly they afford access by means of double locks to the import and export docks. The import dock has a water area of 36 acres, and the export dock an area of 24 acres. Abutting on and around these basins and docks are warehouses, wine and spirit cellars, sheds, wharfs, piling grounds, &c. The two docks are built with brick-work five feet in thickness. Parallel with the export dock there has recently been constructed a new basin, which is termed "the new South Dock." It has monopolized what was formerly the "City canal"—originally constructed at a cost of £133,000. The Company, by providing additional water area on either side of the "canal," have successfully formed a spacious and most convenient new dock. Its length is 2,650 feet, its breadth 450 feet, and there are 16 jetties extending from the northern bank, each 130 feet in length. It is anticipated that this new basin will be an immense assistance in facilitating the business of the Company.

The total expense of the works as originally constructed was £1,200,000. The cost of the new South Dock, which was formally opened on the 5th of March, 1870, is estimated at £500,000. It is stated that in the construction of the South Dock no fewer than sixty-one millions of bricks were used.

The first stone of the "East India Docks" was laid on the 4th of March, 1805. These docks are situate at the eastern extremity of the parish, the principal entrance being in the East India-road. They were constructed by Mr. Rennie and Mr. Ralph Walker, both eminent engineers. The large dock for unloading inwards is 1,460 feet wide by 560 in breadth, and it is considered to be capable of docking 84 vessels of 800 tons burthen. The smaller dock, for unloading outwards, is 760 feet by 520. There is only one entrance to these docks, namely, at Blackwall, and it communicates with an entrance basin 2¾ acres in extent, which affords, by means of locks, admission into both main basins. The docks were opened on the 4th of August, 1806, by the introduction of five ships with valuable cargoes, the property of the East India Company.

In 1866 a Company—the Millwall Freehold Land and Dock Company—purchased 204 acres of land on the Isle of Dogs, with a view of constructing new docks, the plans of which were stated in the prospectus to be "upon a most extensive scale," and were intended to provide the finest dock accommodation in London. These plans were carried out, and in 1868 the "New Millwall Dock" was formally opened. The water area of the principal dock is 32 acres in extent, but it is said to be the intention of the Company to increase this acreage to 52 ; and the remaining 152 acres of the land are devoted to warehouses and wharves. Mr. Fowler was the engineer, and Messrs. Aird & Kelk the builders of the works. According to the reports of the Company, issued half-yearly, it would appear, however, that the gigantic scheme has not met with the success anticipated by its projectors.

Poplar Hospital was founded in July, 1855, by a committee principally composed of gentlemen resident in the locality. It was established for the purpose of affording immediate aid and relief in cases of dangerous accidents ; and being in close proximity to the docks and shipbuilding yards, is a boon of the very greatest magnitude to the working population. It is situate at the extreme east-end of East India Dock-road. The building, which is the property of the East India Dock Company, was formerly used as a Custom-house ; and the hospital authorities now rent it from the Company for £50 per annum—it is scarcely necessary to state that its actual value as a rentable property is considerably more than that sum. Accommodation is provided for 30 in-door patients ; and, in addition to these, medical advice is given to a large number of out-patients, who also, for a few pence, receive medicine, &c. Persons are admitted as in-patients according to the emergency of their case, and under the order of the medical officers ; out-patients are admitted by letters of recommendation, obtainable from subscribers to the institution.   During the past year (1869) no less than 2,391 cases of accident were treated by the medical officers, all of whom, excepting the house-surgeon, afford their services gratuitously.   The total amount of sub-scriptions, &c., received by the hospital authorities last year amounted to £2,577 ; and during the same period the dis-bursements were £1,921 2s. 6½d.   One-fourth of the sum received in 1869 in support of the hospital was contributed by the mechanics and seamen of the neighbourhood.   It is an institution to be commended to all who take an interest in the well-being of their more needy fellow-creatures.

On the north side of East India Dock-road is an institution which has rendered invaluable service to the seafaring men of Great Britain.   We refer to "Green's Sailors' Home."   This establishment was erected in 1841-42 at the sole expense of the late George Green, Esq., of Blackwall Yard, at a cost of no less than £16,000.   The building was erected by Mr. Constable, and accommodation is provided for 180 seamen. Its architectural design is simple, but efficient.   In the centre of the frontage is a portico-entrance, supported by four pillars, and approached by a pathway and broad-treaded steps.   Right and left of the entrance are corridors, the former leading to shipping and other offices, the latter to the portion of the building devoted to domestic and general use.   Mr. Green founded the institution originally for the exclusive accommo-dation of the seamen of his own fleet, and to the reception of these it was devoted for some years; but, upon the solicitation of many friends, he was eventually induced to throw it open for the use of all seamen who chose to express their wish to locate themselves therein during their temporary stay on shore, and it still remains open to all.   It was opened in 1842 without ceremony,—a few gentlemen of Mr. Green's acquaintance met in the large room, and after a prayer had been offered, the worthy founder pronounced the building to be ready for use. After the death of Mr. G. Green, his son Mr. Richard Green exhibited a deep interest in the "Home," and by his benevolent acts and kindly disposition became greatly esteemed by the inhabitants of the parish. He died much lamented in 1862, and was followed to the family grave at the rear of Trinity Chapel, East India-road (also erected at the expense of his late father), by thousands of the parishioners, who, a short time after his decease, erected a monument to his memory at a cost of £1,200. It is to be observed in East India-road, a few yards west of the parish church. Mr. Green is represented sitting in an arm chair, and reclining at his feet is a figure of his favourite Newfoundland Dog. The monument is cast in bronze, and mounted on a pedestal of polished granite, in the front of which, enclosed in a laurel wreath, are simply the words " Richard Green—1866."

The population of the parish of Poplar, according to a census taken in 1811 was 7,708 ; the census of 1831 gave the number as 16,849 ; and according to the last census (1861) the population had increased to 43,529.

Parliamentary, Magisterial, and Parochial Representatives, Clergy, Officers, &c.

The parish is situate in the county of Middlesex, and in the borough of the Tower Hamlets. His Grace the Duke of Wellington, K.G., is *Custos Rotulorum* and Lord Lieutenant of the County, which is represented in the House of Commons by Lord Claud Hamilton and Viscount Enfield. The borough is represented by Acton Smee Ayrton, Esq. (who holds office under the Crown as First Commissioner of Works), and by Joseph D'Aquila Samuda, Esq.

Justices of the Peace : Henry Green, Esq. (chairman of the bench), Blackwall Yard ; J. T. Fletcher, Esq. ; — Charrington, Esq. ; and T. White, Esq.

Coroner for the county in which Poplar is situate : John Humphreys, Esq., Spital-square.

Representative at the Metropolitan Board of Works : Edward Rider Cook, Esq., Bow.

Rector of the Parish : The Rev. T. W. Nowell, the Rectory, Newby Place. Curates : The Rev. R. C. Vaughan, East India-road ; and the Rev. J. Frost, Newby-place.

For Poor-law purposes the parish is united with the adjoining parishes of Bromley and Bow, the whole comprising what is termed the " Poplar Union." The following are the names of the gentlemen elected by the parishioners to sit as Guardians of the poor for the year 1870 : John Young Gibbs, Esq. (vice-chairman), auctioneer and timber merchant, High-street ; William Hickson, Esq., superintendent of the East and West India Docks, Preston's-road ; William Walker, Esq., timber merchant, Regent's Wharf, Millwall ; Alfred A. Cole, Esq., licensed victualler, West India Dock-road ; George Guttridge,

Esq., meat salesman, Montague-place; John Lenanton, Esq., timber merchant, Batson's Wharf, West Ferry-road; George Sadler Esq., licensed victualler, Robinhood-lane; and George Cook, Esq., manufacturing chemist, West Ferry-road. The Poor Law Board nominate three gentlemen to sit with the elected Guardians; the nominated Guardians are: Charles Hampden Wigram, Esq., shipbuilder, Blackwall-yard; John R. Ravenhill, engineer, Glass House-fields; and Thomas Scrutton, Esq., ship-broker, East India Dock-road. Henry Green, Esq., and Henry Green, Jun., Esq., are *ex-officio* members. The chairman of the Board, J. Barringer, Esq., of Upton Villas, Stratford, is one of the representatives of the parish of Bow. Clerk to the Guardians: James R. Collins, Esq., Grosvenor-road, Highbury, and at the Workhouse, Poplar. The Guardians meet every Friday afternoon, at the Workhouse, High-street.

For Sanitary matters the parish is combined with the parishes of Bow and Bromley, the three parishes being denominated the "Poplar District." The District Board of Works consists of 48 members, of which number 28 sit as representatives of the parish of Poplar. Members are elected by and from the Vestrymen of the parish. Edward Coleman, Esq., High-street, Poplar, is chairman of the Board. Clerk: Samuel Jeffries Barth, Esq., the Hermitage, Bromley; Surveyor: Robert Parker, Esq., Avenue-road, Bow. The present offices of the Board are 291, East India Dock-road, but in a few months the business will be transferred to the new offices in course of erection (see page 13).

The Parochial affairs of the parish are managed by three bodies, namely: a Trustee Board, comprised of gentlemen rated on property assessed at not less than £25; a Vestry Board, elected annually by the parishioners under the provisions of Sir Benjamin Hall's Act; and a Board of Vestrymen, possessing the same qualifications as the Trustees, denominated the "Church Vestry." To the first is deputed the task of making and collecting the local rates; the second elect one Churchwarden, the two Overseers, and members of the District Board of Works; and the third body transact all business relating to the parish Church, &c. A second Churchwarden is nominated by the rector, the Rev. T. W. Nowell.

For the ensuing year the following gentlemen have been elected Churchwardens : C. Beaumont, Esq., Brunswick-street, Blackwall ; H. Edgcumbe, Esq., High-street ; and B. A. Beale, Esq.. Shirbutt-street ; and W. H. Bradshaw, Esq., of Strafford-villas, Millwall, have been elected Overseers.   Clerk : W. G. Ceely, Esq., High-street, Poplar.   Temporary offices, 1, Poplar-terrace (see erection of New Town Hall, page 20).

Poor and other Rate Collectors : South District, Mr. J. T. Ceely, 128, High-street ; North District, Mr. E. Glinister, 2, Bow-lane, Poplar.

Assessed Taxes Collectors : North District, Mr. L. Hinton, 236, High-street; South District, Mr. J. C. Riddall, 154, High-street.

The parish is supplied with water by the East London Waterworks Company (incorporated by Act of Parliament). For ordinary house property the Company are entitled to claim payment at the rate of 5 per cent. per annum upon the rental ; where there is an " extra service"—for additional bath-rooms, &c.—a further charge of 4s. per each " extra" per annum is allowed by the Act.   The occupier, and consequently the consumer, is legally the responsible party for the payment of the water-rate.   Complaints should be addressed to the Company's inspector, P. Edinger, Esq., at the Works, Old Ford.

www.ingramcontent.com/pod-product-compliance
Lightning Source LLC
Chambersburg PA
CBHW021621290326
41931CB00047B/1399